ELLA HICKSON

Ella Hickson is an award-winning writer whose work has been performed throughout the UK and abroad. Her most recent plays, *The Writer* and *Oil*, opened at the Almeida Theatre in 2018 and 2017 respectively. In 2013–14 *Wendy & Peter Pan*, adapted from the book by J.M. Barrie, played to wide acclaim at the Royal Shakespeare Company. Other credits include *Riot Girls* (Radio 4), *Boys* (Nuffield Theatre Southampton/Headlong Theatre/HighTide Festival Theatre), *Decade* (Headlong Theatre/St Katharine Docks), *The Authorised Kate Bane* (Grid Iron/Traverse Theatre, Edinburgh), *Rightfully Mine* (Radio 4), *Precious Little Talent* (Trafalgar Studios/Tantrums Productions), *Hot Mess* (Arcola Tent/Tantrums Productions) and *Eight* (Trafalgar Studios/Bedlam Theatre, Edinburgh). In 2011 Ella was the Pearson Writer-in-Residence at the Lyric Theatre Hammersmith and she was the recipient of the 2013 Catherine Johnson Award. She has twice been a MacDowell Fellow. She is developing new work for the National Theatre, the Old Vic and Manhattan Theatre Club. Her short film *Hold On Me* premiered at the 55th BFI London Film Festival. She is also developing various projects for TV and film.

BEN AND MAX RINGHAM

Ben and Max Ringham's work in theatre includes *Berberian Sound Studio* at the Donmar Warehouse; *Tartuffe*, *Ugly Lies the Bone*, *We Want You to Watch*, *Scenes from an Execution*, *Henry IV Parts 1 and 2*, *She Stoops to Conquer* and *The World of Extreme Happiness* at the National; *A Mad World My Masters*, *Queen Anne* (also at the Haymarket) and *Little Eagles* for the RSC; *Love and Information* at Sheffield; *Machinal* at the Almeida; *Present Laughter* at Chichester; *The Wolves* at Stratford East; *Belleville* at the Donmar Warehouse; *The Mighty Walzer*, *Parliament Square* and *Our Town* at the Royal Exchange; *Twilight Song* at Park Theatre; *Gloria* at Hampstead; *Pygmalion* for Headlong at West Yorkshire Playhouse and Nuffield; *Killer* (Off-Westend Awards Best Sound Designer Winner), and *The Pitchfork Disney* at Shoreditch Town Hall; *Lunch and The Bow of Ulysses*, *The Hothouse*, *The Maids* and *Apologia* at Trafalgar Studios;

After Miss Julie and *The School for Scandal* at Theatre Royal Bath; *The Girl on the Train* on UK tour; *Strangers on a Train* and *Gaslight* for the Ambassador Theatre Group; *The Government Inspector* and *Tartuffe* at Birmingham REP; *Raz* at Assembly and Riverside Studios; *Ben Hur*, *Paper Dolls*, *Multitudes* and *A Wolf in Snakeskin Shoes* at the Tricycle; *Ah, Wilderness!* and *La Musica* at the Young Vic; *Richard III* and *The Ruling Class* for Trafalgar Transformed; *The Walworth Farce* at the Olympia, Dublin; *NSFW*, *2071* and *Adler and Gibb* at the Royal Court; *Minetti* at the Edinburgh International Festival; *Dawn French* and *Fiction* on UK tour; *A Midsummer Night's Dream* for the Michael Grandage Company; *The Pride* (Best Overall Achievement in an Affiliate Theatre Laurence Olivier Award Winner, as part of the creative team) at the Royal Court, Trafalgar Studios and on UK tour; *Lungs* at Schaubühne, Berlin; *Ring* (Off-Westend Awards Best Sound Designer Winner) at Battersea Arts Centre and UK tour; *The Motor Show* at LIFT; *The Painkiller* at the Lyric, Belfast; *My City* at the Almeida; *The History Boys*, *Boeing Boeing*, *A Taste of Honey*, *An Enemy of the People*, *Racing Demon* and *Hamlet* at Sheffield Crucible; *The Electric Hotel* for Fuel and Sadler's Wells; *Glorious* for Rajni Shah Productions; *Les Parents Terribles* for the Donmar at Trafalgar Studios; *Phaedra* and *Polar Bears* at the Donmar Warehouse; *Piaf* (Best Sound Design Olivier Award nomination) at the Donmar Warehouse, Vaudeville and in Buenos Aires; *All About My Mother*, *Democracy* (also at Sheffield Crucible) and *The Duchess of Malfi* at the Old Vic; *Contains Violence* at the Lyric, Hammersmith; *The Caretaker* at the Sheffield Crucible, the Tricycle and on UK tour; *The Architects*, *Amato Saltone*, *What If…?*, *Tropicana*, *Dance Bear Dance* and *The Ballad of Bobby Francois* for Shunt; *The Full Monty* (also at Sheffield Theatres), *What the Butler Saw*, *Blithe Spirit* (also on US tour), *The Lover/The Collection*, *Three Days of Rain*, *The Ladykillers* (also on UK tour; Best Sound Design Olivier Award nomination); *The Little Dog Laughed*, *The Miser*, *Pinter at the Pinter*, *The Dresser*, *King Lear* (also at Chichester), *Doctor Faustus*, *Quiz* (also at Chichester) and *Perfect Nonsense* in the West End. Other composition/sound design work includes *Frida Kahlo Making Herself Up* at the V&A; *Mirror Maze* and *Room 2022* with Es Devlin; *Rembrandt The Late Works* at the National Gallery; *The Inspection Chamber* for Alexa; BBC Research and Development; and *Papa Sangre II* – a sound-based IOS game for Somethin' Else (IMGA Excellence in Sound Design Award Winner). Ben and Max Ringham are also the co-creators of Wiretapper, a company creating sound-based performance in public spaces.

ANNA

Created by Ella Hickson,
Ben and Max Ringham

NICK HERN BOOKS

London
www.nickhernbooks.co.uk

A Nick Hern Book

ANNA first published as a paperback original in Great Britain in 2019
by Nick Hern Books Limited, The Glasshouse, 49a Goldhawk Road, London
W12 8QP

ANNA copyright © 2019 Ella Hickson
Introduction copyright © 2019 Ella Hickson

Ella Hickson has asserted her right to be identified as the author of this work

Cover photography (Phoebe Fox) by Sebastian Nevols; art direction and design
by National Theatre Graphic Design Studio.

Designed and typeset by Nick Hern Books, London
Printed in the UK by Mimeo Ltd, Huntingdon, Cambridgeshire PE29 6XX

A CIP catalogue record for this book is available from the British Library

ISBN   978 1 84842 858 4

Introduction
Ella Hickson

Binaural sound is a method of recording sound that uses two microphones arranged to offer the listener a stereo-sound sensation. Wearing individual headphones, the audience get a 'sound close-up'. They listen from the 'point of hearing' of one character; in this case, Anna.

The audience of the original National Theatre production heard the play through Anna – but they saw it through the glass fourth wall of a replica 1968 P2 Plattenbau apartment in East Berlin. The ground-plan of this set, designed by Vicki Mortimer and drawn by Robert Perkins, appears on page vii. In our production, as much of the interior, costume and props were true to period as possible. This made the set an instrument that was able to create the audio environment of 1968 East Berlin: the sound of Communism.

Receiving the show through the audio perspective of a single character necessitates that some of the script is seen and not heard (and other sections are heard and not seen). I would encourage any future production to be rigorous with all action whether on or off mic; all ten characters have an arc, motivation and resolution – the process should be egalitarian.

Portions of the script are divided into two, three or four columns, representing simultaneous action in different places. When there are two columns with the same heading, this indicates separate action stage-left and stage-right of the same room. The script should be read down the page, with any lines horizontally aligned being spoken simultaneously.

The audience can hear everything printed in bold (which is Anna's audio track); <u>anything that is underlined can be partially heard or is heard at a distance</u>; and anything that is neither bold nor underlined isn't heard at all.

The staging of this requires vocal control, precise timing, physical meticulousness amd technical coordination. This is hugely demanding on all members of the cast and crew. I feel exceptionally lucky to have been part of a team that could deal with these demands, and very proud of the work we've made as a result.

'It's just I've spent thirty-five years being heard.' Michael Gould (Dieter Bourmer in the original production)*

* *Michael Gould would like it to be known that he said this in jest.*

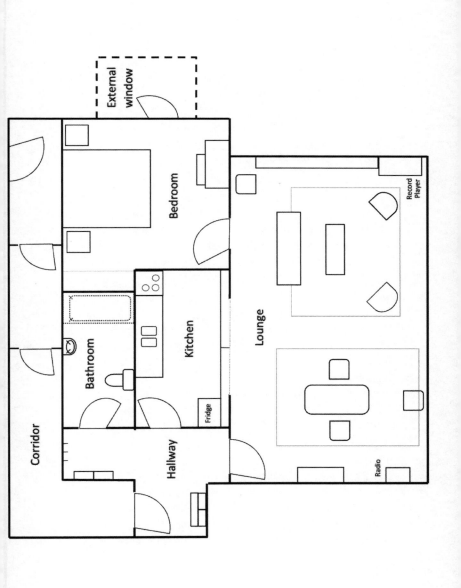

External window

Bedroom

Corridor

Bathroom

Kitchen

Fridge

Hallway

Lounge

Radio

Record Player

ANNA was first performed in the Dorfman auditorium of the National Theatre, London, on 21 May 2019 (previews from 11 May). The cast, in alphabetical order, was as follows:

MARION BOURMER	Nathalie Armin
HANS WEBER	Paul Bazely
CHRISTIAN NEUMANN	Max Bennett
PETER SCHMIDT	Jamie Bradley
ANNA WEBER	Phoebe Fox
DIETER BOURMER	Michael Gould
SOPHIE MUNDT	Georgia Landers
ELENA HILLENBRAND	Diana Quick
FREDERICKA (FRED) ZIEGLER	Lara Rossi
KARL WOLF	Dwane Walcott

Director	Natalie Abrahami
Writer	Ella Hickson
Composition and Sound Design	Ben and Max Ringham
Set and Costume Designer	Vicki Mortimer
Lighting Designer	Jon Clark
Movement Director	Anna Morrissey
Associate Lighting Designer	Ben Jacobs
Associate Movement Director	Laura Cubitt
Company Voice Work	Stevie Rickard
Staff Director	Anthony Lau

Project Producer	Christine Gettins
Production Manager	Tom Lee
Associate Production Manager	Nick Flintoff
Casting	Alastair Coomer CDG
Stage Manager	Andrew Speed
Deputy Stage Manager	Vicky Eames
Assistant Stage Manager	Robert Perkins

ANNA

For Ben, Max and Trevor

Vergangenheitsbewältigung (noun: German):
Overcoming the past.

'This feeling needs a stickle-brick word: I can only describe it as horror-romance. The romance comes from the dream of a better world the German Communists wanted to build out of the ashes of their Nazi past. The horror comes from what they did in its name.'

Stasiland, Anna Funder

Characters

DIETER BOURMER, *fifty-seven, long-serving factory employee, life and soul of the party but, these days, struggling. Intensely loyal with a huge heart*

MARION BOURMER, *fifty, factory head secretary for decades, low heels, knee-length skirt, robust, kind. Essential to everyone but rarely reminded of it*

ELENA HILLENBRAND, *sixty-eight, impressive, restrained, you can only imagine what she's lived through*

SOPHIE MUNDT, *twenty-five, new to Marion's secretarial pool; eager and upright. Hasn't yet seen what she needs to see to fully understand the world but she's not stupid. Seeking, nervous*

CHRISTIAN NEUMANN, *thirty-seven, Aryan – repressed, seemingly affable, carries a lust for control like the faint taste of blood in his mouth. Exciting to be around*

PETER SCHMIDT, *thirty-eight, intellectual, doctor-turned-researcher at Humboldt University. Old friends with Christian Neumann; alert, conscious, aware. Holds information*

ANNA WEBER, *thirty-five, slight, keenly intelligent, a strong interior world, reserved but capable of great joy. Holds an anxiety; fears the loss of control*

HANS WEBER, *thirty-nine, seems older. Straight-forward, uncomplicated, loyal. Warm. Has never confronted/is unaware of his own weaknesses; good to be around, had dreams of being a musician – but long-forgotten*

KARL WOLF, *thirty, has the sense of young buck about him; ex-sports star, bright, ambitious*

FREDERICKA (FRED) ZIEGLER, *thirty-three, sane, rational, teacher, Anna's best friend. Upbeat but feels hurt in some way*

Setting

February. A flat. P2. Plattenbau; Leninplatz. 1968.

The building is new. The way of living is new. They are delighted.

The front wall gives us full visual access to the sitting room.

Stage-left is a sofa, an armchair, a seating area. Stage-right is a dining area; a table, a sideboard, a record player. Across the back wall of the sitting room, one door, stage-left, that leads into Hans and Anna's bedroom; we have partial visual access to this room. Next – a large kitchen hatch – through which we can see the majority of the kitchen. Next, stage-right, a door that opens into the hallway; the hallway contains – a small side table, the front door to the apartment, access to the kitchen and access to the bathroom.

This text went to press before the end of rehearsals and so may differ slightly from the play as performed.

ANNA ARRIVES HOME FROM WORK

ANNA *arrives home from work.*

ANNA *takes her keys out of her pocket and unlocks the front door.*

ANNA *opens the front door – closes it behind her – puts her keys down on the hall table, she's precise and particular.*

ANNA *turns on the hall light, we can see her in half-shadow. The rest of the apartment appears, only fractionally, in the gloom.*

ANNA *enters the sitting room, puts a stack of marking down on the dining-room table, and a shopping bag. The shopping bag contains snacks.*

ANNA *heads to the bookcase – takes a pack of cigarettes off the shelf – takes one out, lights it. Breathes it in, relaxes, exhales. Tests the air, waits.*

The room is alive: we hear the clock, the distant street, people upstairs, the hum of the lights, the muffled sound of the kitchen; life – incredibly close, very far.

ANNA *leaves her cigarette in the ashtray, turns on the radio, listens a moment. East German news. She checks her watch. She moves quicker now, with purpose, towards the bedroom when…*

The telephone rings. ANNA stops. Stares at the telephone.

She returns to the sideboard, turns off the radio. Picks up the telephone.

—

ANNA. **Hello.**

FEMALE VOICE. Hello.

ANNA. Hello?

FEMALE VOICE. Hello.

ANNA. Hello.

ANNA *puts the telephone down.*

ANNA *turns upstage and heads into the bedroom.*

ANNA *opens the window.*

We can see her, in the half-light, her silhouette – as she gets changed; there's something filmic, privileged – yet partial – about our access.

ANNA *takes off her coat. Takes off her dress. She's careful.*

ANNA *changes.*

ANNA *heads into the bathroom.*

ANNA *breathes, hums under her breath.*

ANNA *runs the tap.*

ANNA *taps her toothbrush on the side of the sink.*

ANNA *brushes her teeth.*

A figure, hidden in the darkness, appears from behind the sitting-room door.

The figure approaches the bathroom.

8

The figure reaches into his pocket.

The figure exits the flat – slamming the door behind it.

The figure exits the flat; throws toothbrush in the sink – exits the bathroom.

ANNA thinks she hears something; throws toothbrush in the sink – exits the bathroom.

ANNA opens the front door.

A distant cough.

No one is there.

ANNA enters the corridor.

Hello?

ANNA hears the lift closing and descending.

ANNA closes the door. Breathes out.

ANNA listens – she can hear footsteps in the outside hall, they are approaching the flat.

A figure moves past the window to the internal corridor. She watches, closely.

The clanking sound of glass against glass.

ANNA waits at the door. Her breathing quickens, someone at the front door.

ANNA stares at the front door.

The front door opens.

HANS opens the front door. ANNA is standing, in the half-dark, staring at the door.

HANS ARRIVES HOME FROM WORK

HANS. Hi.

ANNA. Hi.

HANS. Are you okay?

ANNA. Yes.

HANS. What are you doing standing in the dark?

ANNA. I thought I heard someone in the hallway.

HANS. You did. It was me.

ANNA (*grinning*). I'm excited.

HANS. What are you excited about?

ANNA takes HANS by the arm – pulls him inside.

ANNA. Tonight. The party. (*Takes his coat.*) How was today? Did they shower you with praise?

ANNA moves aside and lets him past.

HANS. There was a small amount of fuss made.

ANNA (*as he passes, laughs*). Section manager.

HANS walks a little fancy, like he's pleased with himself – to the table, to put down his crate of food/booze. ANNA watches, laughs.

You think that's how section managers walk?

10

HANS. I should know.

HANS *takes a record out of the crate.*

Ta-dah.

ANNA. What's that?

HANS. Some very trendy music for my very trendy wife.

ANNA. It's for me is it?

HANS *puts the record on.*

I thought we were putting the bonus towards a television?

HANS. It's the Manfred Ludwig Septet. It's the one with Konrad Bauer playing the trombone.

ANNA, *watches, charmed.* HANS *puts the record on – he starts to dance. He dances towards her, she laughs.*

They're really very good.

ANNA. Very sophisticated.

HANS *(takes her, spins her round).* I'm a sophisticated guy.

She laughs. They dance – at some distance, it's cool – upbeat, trendy, they're actually quite good.

I like this dress.

ANNA. This dress likes you.

HANS. Where did you get it? The dress?

ANNA. I don't think you really care where I got it. I think you only care about when I get out of it.

They dance – HANS does a trombone solo in her ear.

They kiss.

We're going to be late. Your colleagues are going to think I'm disorganised.

HANS. You smell good.

Face kissing. HANS goes for the zip on ANNA's dress – she wriggles, suddenly nervous, and breaks away.

ANNA. Oi! There's no time for that, Mr Section Manager. You need to shave.

HANS. I need to shave? You need to shave.

HANS slaps ANNA's bum.

ANNA cuts away and heads into the kitchen.

ANNA. Go and shave.

HANS heads into the bathroom – he shaves.

ANNA at the fridge, breath – she does a shot from a shot glass.

Knock at the door.

ANNA opens the door.

FRED. You left your marking at school.

ANNA. Thank you. (*Exhales.*) I'm all over the place today.

FRED. Nice dress.

ANNA. It's for this party for Hans and his workmates.

12

FRED. Make sure you keep it down, alright?

Laugh.

ANNA. You doing anything fun?

FRED. No, I'm shattered. I just passed Elena Hillenbrand in the street. She's on her way up.

ANNA. Hillenbrand?

FRED. Your old neighbour. I just saw her in the lobby.

ANNA. She can't be here.

FRED. Why?

ANNA. Her husband – Robert, got – he's been – arrested.

FRED. Okay.

ANNA. Hans' new boss is coming this evening and he's a Party member and /

FRED. / Anna?

ANNA. Sorry – I –

FRED. I don't really want to – get involved in all that.

ANNA. Yes, I know. Sorry. I –

FRED *walks to the door.*

FRED. Oh, Tuesday.

ANNA. Yes?

FRED. You said you were free.

ANNA. I am.

FRED. I thought you might come for a drink and meet – my new –

ANNA (*fun*). Yeees?

FRED. Uh – man person.

ANNA. Man person?

FRED. I just want someone to you know /

ANNA. / to check he's not a psychopath?

FRED. Correct.

ANNA. I look forward to it. (*Kisses her.*)

HANS (*kicks open the door and shouts from bathroom*). Anna, can you iron my shirt?

ANNA. Just think if it works out – you too could be ironing someone's shirt on a Friday night.

    HANS *comes out of the bathroom.*

HANS. Fred!

FRED. I'm leaving – before your mates get here and things really kick off.

    FRED *laughs, leaves.*

HANS. You're missing out.

ANNA. You want a drink? We'll just have one before everyone arrives.

13

ANNA *looks at* HANS. HANS *catches her eye. They talk through the kitchen hatch –* HANS' *voice sounds far away.* ANNA *is partially visible – we zoom in.*

Did they do a presentation at work?

HANS. After lunch, everyone was called onto the factory floor and I was asked to say something.

ANNA. A word from the new section manager?

HANS. Yes.

ANNA. Look at you grinning.

HANS. Don't mock me.

ANNA. I'm not. I'm proud of you.

HANS. Herr Neumann called me into his office afterwards and we had some drinks. I felt like – such a – it was nice. The boss's office.

ANNA. What did you talk about?

HANS. Production targets – that sort of thing.

ANNA. Is that all?

HANS. Yeah.

HANS *looks down at the books on the table, then back at* ANNA *in the kitchen as she makes the shots. He loves her.* ANNA *is breathing heavily, trying to calm down.* HANS *reads a little.* ANNA *takes a shot, hidden from* HANS.

Is this your marking? It doesn't look like economics.

ANNA. Don't mess around with them. They're in alphabetical order.

HANS. 'At the weekend, my neighbours and I take the car and head to the Oberhoff for a camping trip. The trees are a vivid green. The tent is surprisingly spacious.' (*Laughs.*) He's not Goethe.

ANNA. They're economics students.

HANS. Is it a euphemism? Having a spacious tent?

ANNA. Put them down. It's an invasion of privacy.

She hands him the glass – she fills it.

They're describing the world created by their ideal economic model.

HANS. His utopia is a spacious tent? This is the next generation?

ANNA. I don't know. I quite like a spacious tent.

They laugh – neither really knowing what it means.

HANS. What does that mean?

ANNA. I don't really know.

HANS. Say economic model again.

ANNA. Shut up and drink your schnapps.

HANS. Just say it once more. Say economic model whilst you're in that dress.

ANNA *raises her glass. HANS knocks his back, puts his glass down and grabs* ANNA, *wanting to dance – she wiggles out.*

ANNA. Are you going to change?

HANS. Show me your spacious tent.

15

ANNA. You need to put a clean shirt on and put the things that need to be put into the bowls, into the bowls.

She throws these things out of the crate that HANS brought home with him.

HANS. Who's the section manager now?

ANNA. Me.

HANS takes the snacks and starts to put them out. ANNA takes the crate back through to the kitchen.

HANS. What happened last night?

ANNA clatters the crate.

ANNA. What do you mean?

HANS. I woke up and you weren't there.

ANNA. Nothing.

HANS. What were you doing?

Buzzer.

ANNA. Who is that?

VOICE. Hello!

ANNA. That's not one of your friends, get the door. Hans? Remember.

HANS. What?

ANNA kisses HANS.

HANS cuts past ANNA and opens the door.

ELENA ARRIVES

ELENA, *simultaneously unassuming and impressive.*

HANS. Elena?

ANNA *goes into the kitchen.*

ELENA. Hello Hans. Can I come in?

ANNA. Hans is having friends from work round this evening.

ELENA. I wondered if I could come in and get warm.

ANNA. Why are you so cold? Come in, come in. Make yourself comfortable. I have to finish getting ready.

ELENA. I can't lift the coal up from the basement without Robert. None of the neighbours will help me any more.

Beat.

ANNA. You should have rung.

ELENA. I didn't want to be a nuisance. I know you're busy – you have busy lives.

HANS *is standing in the sitting room, watching.* ELENA *comes through towards the dining table. Once* ELENA *is past and into the sitting room,* HANS *whispers to* ANNA.

HANS. She can't be here when Herr Neumann gets here.

ANNA *tries to move away.*

Her husband has just been arrested.

17

ANNA. It'll be fine.

HANS. Anna?

ELENA. This place, it looks amazing. It really looks like those pictures in the magazines; cheerful children and a charming woman in an apron. Maybe that's you, Anna?

ANNA. I don't think so. Do you want some schnapps? Help you warm up?

ELENA. I'll have coffee, if you have some?

ANNA. Hans?

HANS (*in the kitchen*). Sure.

HANS *watches – concerned. HANS makes the coffee. He stares at the two women.*

ANNA *and* ELENA *go to the window.*

ANNA. We can see your kitchen light from our window.

ANNA *points it out.*

ELENA. Don't you get dizzy at this height?

ANNA (*whispered*). You know the great thing about Berlin. It's all mine.

ELENA (*quietly*). You okay?

ANNA (*quietly*). Fine. You?

ELENA (*quietly*). Fine. Yes. Thank you.

ANNA *stands at the window a little while, she watches.* ELENA *returns upstage to talk to* HANS *at the hatch. We don't hear it.*

If you wash it out like that, the coffee grounds will go everywhere.

HANS *ignores it.*

Hans?

ANNA *checks her watch.*

HANS. Why don't I do your coal now?

ELENA. Do you mind if I stay up here for a while?

HANS. Of course. I was just trying to help.

ANNA *makes her way back over to the kitchen, she catches this conversation.*

ELENA. She told me Herr Neumann has made you section manager.

HANS. Who?

ELENA. Anna.

HANS. When did she tell you that?

ELENA. On the phone. Is he a good guy? He promoted you, so I guess you like him.

Pause. ANNA *and* HANS *say nothing.*

It's amazing they found someone to replace Robert so quickly after he disappeared.

19

Pause. Sound. The kettle rising – ANNA and HANS stop in the space.

ANNA. Elena.

ELENA. What's wrong? I'm not allowed to say disappeared?

No response.

My husband, your friend your employer has disappeared, Hans?

No response.

HANS *looks at* ANNA.

ANNA. Shall we get you your coffee?

ELENA. I'm not sure I want it any more.

HANS *moves out of the kitchen to go and put another record on.*

Are you putting music on?

HANS. A little. Sure.

ELENA. That's a shame. I love it here. I like the silence. It's incredible. How quiet it is up here.

Doorbell.

You can hardly hear a thing. It's a racket down on the street.

A knock at the door.

Pause – they all freeze.

HANS (*shouting through*). **That'll be our guests.** (*To* ELENA.) If you'll excuse me a moment.

HANS *comes to the door.* ANNA *freezes in the kitchen.* ELENA *looks back to check on her.*

ANNA. **We're not ready. I haven't got all of the food out.**

HANS. **It's okay. They're our friends, Anna. Ca–**

ANNA. **Don't tell me to calm down.**

ANNA *opens the door.*

21

THE GANG ARRIVE

ANNA. I'll do it – you go and change your shirt.

ANNA nips past HANS and opens the door – a wall of noise hits her – 'congratuuuallations' – laughter, the gang slightly fuck up the joke.

It's not Hans.

HANS. I'm here! I'm here!

Second whoop when HANS arrives at the door.

DIETER. We had it all prepared.

MARION. Hi!

DIETER. Hi!

ANNA. Come in, come in, come in – you horrible lot.

HALLWAY

KARL darts past with the beer keg.

HANS. Karl! Ow! Karl.

ANNA tries to kiss him and misses. DIETER enters – shakes HANS' hand, slaps him on the back, doesn't let go.

HALLWAY

MARION, with platters.

MARION. Hi love.

ANNA. Hi Marion.

MARION and ANNA kiss.

(To KARL.) Don't put that on the table without something underneath it! *(They kiss.)*

SITTING ROOM

ELENA. Karl Wolf!

KARL runs in with the keg and tries to get it down.

KARL. Sorry, it's really heavy!

ELENA. Karl.

DIETER. Man of the hour, how you doing?

HANS. Good, thanks. Nice to see you.

ANNA. Hi Dieter.

DIETER. Hi little lady (*Loud kiss.*) Mwah.

ANNA. Do you want me to take those?

DIETER. Ta.

ANNA *takes bottles from DIETER and moves into the sitting room.*

DIETER. It's a nice place, isn't it? Hans?

HANS. Yes.

DIETER. Saying what a nice place it is.

HANS. Come through, come through. Marion, are you alright in there?

MARION. Yes, yes – I'm fine, go on through. Dieter – where did you put the cake?

MARION *organises food – sorts dishes in the kitchen.*

Dieter?

MARION. Hi. Where do you want this?

ANNA. There's space in the kitchen. I'll come through in a second.

MARION. It's okay. I can work it out. My god, they're tiny these kitchens. How do you get anything done in here?

SOPHIE *waits with the cheese hedgehog.*

HANS. Sophie? It's Sophie, right?

SOPHIE. Yes. I hope you don't mind my coming along. Marion said I should, good chance to get to meet everyone.

HANS. Of course, of course – everyone is welcome. Come on in.

SOPHIE *heads into the sitting room.*

KARL. Shit, Frau Hillenbrand.

ELENA. How are you my lad? It's so nice to see you.

KARL. Yeah, I'm good thanks.

They greet.

ANNA *moves into the sitting room.*

ANNA. Karl, can you make sure something is under that, it's going to mark the tablecloth. Karl, you remember Elena.

ELENA. Hello Karl.

KARL. Hi Frau Weber. (*Kiss.*)

ANNA. Less charm, more placemat, Karl. Hans? Can you take people's coats?

KARL. Frau Weber? Frau Weber?

23

SITTING ROOM

DIETER. There! They're big, aren't they?

HANS. The ones on the other side are much bigger.

ANNA. **You've seen flats like this before, Dieter.**

DIETER. You're the first two I know who got one. Lucky buggers.

HANS. We've been on the list for five years. Then all of a sudden /

DIETER. / Jesus – look, just gets bigger and bigger.

HANS. Yeah, it's nice.

DIETER. Great view. Where are the beer glasses, Hans?

HANS *moves to put on some more music.*

KARL. What the hell is this?

HANS. It's the Manfred Ludwig Septet. I won't hear it – that stuff you listen to /

SITTING ROOM

KARL *gives ANNA flowers.*

ANNA. **Come on, Karl. I'm not your mother, call me Anna. Thank you for the flowers. Let me take your coat. Can I get you a beer?**

ANNA *takes his coat.*

KARL *organises the crate.*

(To MARION, kitchen.) **Are you okay? Can you put these in water?**

SITTING ROOM

ELENA. Are you alright there, love?

SOPHIE. I brought this for Frau Weber.

ELENA. **Anna?**

ANNA. Yes, everything okay?

ELENA. **This young lady wanted your attention.**

ANNA. **Hi there.** (*Aside, passing KARL's coat.*) **/ Hans, Hans – take this.**

SOPHIE. **/ Hi, I'm Sophie, I'm the new secretary, Marion invited me – I brought a cheese hedgehog.**

ANNA. **So, you did.**

SOPHIE. **It's half a melon and you put cocktail sticks with cheese /**

ANNA. **/ Shall we put it on the table?** (*Puts the hedgehog down.*)

SOPHIE. **Lovely to meet you.**

KARL. / You're basically dead.

DIETER. Oi, don't give him lip. What is it?

HANS. Manfred Ludwig Septet.

DIETER. You still support Dresden Dynamo?

KARL. Berlin.

HANS (*laughs*). Glory hunter.

KARL. They're just better.

DIETER. Karl's loyalties go wherever the Oberliga goes.

HANS. All okay?

ANNA (*kisses him*). Yes. Is everyone happy? Does anyone want anything they don't have?

KARL *moves across to* SOPHIE *and* ELENA.

HANS. Marion, can you pass me the glasses? They're – no, the big ones for beer. Yeah – there.

MARION. Do you know how I turn this thing on? I hate these electric things –

ANNA *gets a vase from the sideboard for* MARION.

ANNA. Dieter? Have you got a drink? (*Opens bottle.*)

DIETER. We're just getting some glasses.

ANNA. Can I take your coat?

DIETER. I'll keep it, this shirt shows the sweat.

HANS *gets the glasses from the hatch.* MARION *hands them to him.*

(*Shouting.*) Marion! Marion!

HANS. Don't bellow at the woman. I'll get them.

HANS *gets glasses.* DIETER *grabs* ANNA *onto sofa.*

ANNA. No! I'm /

DIETER. / Tell me how you are.

ANNA *tries to stand.*

ANNA. I've got to get things ready.

ANNA. And you – Elena, will you make sure Sophie has a drink?

ELENA. Of course.

SOPHIE. I'm okay for a drink for now. What did you say your name was?

ELENA. Hillenbrand, my husband used to run the factory.

SOPHIE. Oh. He interviewed me. I thought he was really nice.

ELENA. He is a kind man.

KARL. He gave me my first job.

KARL *goes for the hedgehog.*

KARL. What is it?

SOPHIE. A hedgehog.

you never know when they're on and then /

HANS. I'll do it – one second.

HANS goes round into the kitchen to show MARION.

KITCHEN

HANS. It was alright when I was making the coffee.

MARION. I'm going to put them in the oven.

ANNA. What is it?

DIETER. **Don't make me talk to anyone else, I hate them.**

ANNA. **You love them.**

DIETER. **I love you.**

ANNA. **Creep. (***Kisses him.***)**

DIETER. **You met the new boss man, yet?**

ANNA. **No. What's he like? (***Pause.***)**

DIETER. **Handsome. Terrible kisser.**

ANNA laughs, slaps DIETER playfully.

ANNA. **You're my favourite. (***To HANS.***) Out, out! Hans – out! Get out of my kitchen, get out!**

ANNA crosses into the kitchen.

KARL. Does it kill him if I take out one of his spines,

SOPHIE *laughs.*

Oh look, he's coming apart. Ow, ow – don't kill me, don't kill me.

ELENA. Don't nick all the cheese, you toad.

How are things, Karl?

KARL. Good thanks.

ELENA. Are you keeping okay? Looking after yourself.

KARL. Sure. I'm working electrics.

ELENA. Is that interesting? It might mean promotion.

DIETER. I'm not sure it does.

ELENA. Hi there, Dieter.

DIETER *swigs his beer.*

DIETER. Hi.

ELENA. You don't want to talk to me?

DIETER. Of course, how are you?

MARION. Meatballs.

ANNA *enters kitchen.*

ANNA. Do them on the hob.

MARION. Is that Elena Hillenbrand?

ANNA. Yes.

MARION. Right.

ANNA (*whilst fiddling with the hob*). There, hob on. You pair of dolts.

MARION. Anna?

ANNA. That's a beautiful cake, Marion – it must have taken hours. (*Pause.*)

Doorbell.

ANNA. That'll be Herr Neumann, Hans. Open the door. Hans?

HALLWAY

KARL. Do you want me to get it?

DIETER. No, I'll get it.

HANS. No, you're fine.

They greet one another.

You want another beer, Karl?

DIETER *throws nibbles in his mouth and watches the door.*

KARL *is involved, talking to SOPHIE.*

DIETER *crosses to the drinks table.*

Doorbell.

KITCHEN

MARION. He thinks you're pretty.

ANNA. Who?

MARION. Herr Neumann.

ANNA. That's impossible, I've never met him.

27

HANS *does his hair in the mirror.*

DIETER. He's doing his hair! You've already got the promotion. You trying to get laid as well?

HANS *opens the door.*

NEUMANN. Hans Weber!

HANS. Neumann. What time do you call this?

NEUMANN. We took the bike. This one made me drive like a grandmother. Hans, this is my old university pal – Peter Schmidt.

SCHMIDT. Hi, hi – it's great to meet you. A real pleasure. Hi.

HANS. Come in, come in – some folks are already here.

NEUMANN. I hope we're not late.

HANS. No, no not at all. Let me take your coats.

HANS *takes* SCHMIDT *through to the sitting room.*

ANNA *goes to the door – we can hear her breathing, fast.*

ELENA (*in the door of the sitting room*). Okay. All okay?

ANNA. Mm-hmmm.

ELENA *retreats – back over into the sitting room – towards the record player.*

ANNA *cuts into the sitting room. Removes the crate from the table and unpacks the bottles.*

KARL. Did you buy the melon?

SOPHIE. Yes.

KARL. Which cost –?

SOPHIE. It's nice to make an effort.

KARL. And you made it into a hedgehog?

SOPHIE. I saw it in *Sibylle*. It's a magazine.

ELENA. Karl knows it's a magazine.

KARL. Yeah. (*He doesn't know.*)

SOPHIE. Do you know it's a magazine? (*Smiles.*) I'm not sure he does know it's a magazine.

SCHMIDT *is introduced to* DIETER *and* KARL.

THE ARRIVAL OF NEUMANN / THE BUMP

SITTING ROOM	SITTING ROOM	KITCHEN
ANNA *bends down to put bottles away.* NEUMANN *approaches the table.*	HANS *and* SCHMIDT *enter.*	
	SCHMIDT. Hi there, I'm Dr Peter Schmidt.	
NEUMANN. Frau Weber. Is it?	DIETER. Dieter Bourmer. This is Karl – Karl Wolf.	
ANNA. Yes.	SCHMIDT. Peter Schmidt.	
NEUMANN. Herr Neumann, I'm your husband's new boss. I'm so pleased to meet you, Hans /	KARL. Hi.	
ANNA. / I know you –	DIETER. That's my wife, Marion – This is uh –	MARION. Hi there.
NEUMANN. Uh –	SOPHIE. Sophie.	
ANNA. Max. You look just like, Max Becker.	DIETER. Yes, Sophie. Our new secretary. Sorry.	
NEUMANN. Who's Max Becker?	SCHMIDT. I'm a friend of Herr Neumann's from university.	DIETER *comes to the kitchen hatch.*
ANNA. Sorry – we knew each other as children. He was my god, you look just like him /	SOPHIE. Did you say you were a doctor?	DIETER. Can I have a meatball?
	SCHMIDT. Yes.	MARION. No, they're not ready.
NEUMANN. / I'm Christian Neumann. I'm sorry – I really don't think we've met.	KARL. Do I – I feel like we've met.	DIETER. They smell ready.
	KARL *puts a record on.*	MARION. Well they're not.

29

ANNA. Okay, will you excuse me?

ANNA *cuts across to the sofa area.*

HANS. Anna? Anna! You two, come and join us. Herr Neumann – can we get you a drink. Anna – this is Dr Schmidt a friend of Herr Neumann's from university. He works at the Humbolt.

HANS *enters – cuts through KARL and SCHMIDT.*

HANS (*introduces SCHMIDT to ELENA*). And this is Elena Hillenbrand – who uh –

ELENA. I live nearby.

HANS. Elena used to be our neighbour when we lived across the road. Can I get you a drink of anything?

SCHMIDT. I'll have a beer if you've got one, thanks. It's a great place.

HANS. Thanks, thanks – we've been really lucky. We feel very lucky. It's a real – one of these? (*Re: beer.*)

SCHMIDT. That's great, thanks.

[*Concurrent A.*]

KARL *and SOPHIE go to the window.*

KARL. I live just there.

SOPHIE. Oh, that's funny, me too. The other side of the church.

DIETER *loiters by the hatch.*

Go and say hello to Neumann.

DIETER. I'm talking to you.

MARION. No, you're not – go.

KARL. Can I get you a drink?

KARL *gets SOPHIE a drink.*

I like your dress. Who made it?

SOPHIE. My mum made it from a pattern in *Pramo.*

DIETER *goes and sits by the record player. MARION joins him.*

ANNA. Lovely to meet you.

Meanwhile NEUMANN goes over into the group.

SCHMIDT. I hope you don't mind my coming along.

ANNA. No, not at all – you can pop your coat – just over – yes that's it.

NEUMANN. How did you get here so fast. Good to see you.

Laughs.

ANNA. Christian – this is Elena Hillenbrand. She's um – an old friend of mine.

Beat – the room freezes.

NEUMANN. Lovely to meet you.

ELENA *half offers a hand – retracts it. NEUMANN whispers – unheard – to HANS ('What is Elena Hillenbrand doing here?')*

Beat.

ELENA. Can I get you a drink?

KARL. That's close.

SOPHIE. What are you doing?

KARL. Dancing. You don't want to dance?

SOPHIE. The boss is here.

Silence.

KARL. So?

SOPHIE. I don't want him to see me dance.

KARL. But I bet you look great when you dance.

SOPHIE. That's not the point. Look, he's right there, stop it.

[*Concurrent B.*]

HANS. Did you come on Neumann's bike?

SCHMIDT. Yeah. Still can't feel my fingers.

HANS. Cold?

SCHMIDT. Freezing.

MARION. You going to take that jacket off?

DIETER. Leave me alone.

DIETER *pulls away, annoyed.*

Silence.

MARION. Oi.

DIETER. Stop pestering me.

MARION. Dieter?

DIETER. What?

The both stare at NEUMANN and ELENA.

MARION. What are they talking about?

DIETER. Pass me a pretzel.

DIETER *shouts over the table.*

KARL *persuades SOPHIE to dance a little.*

NEUMANN. No.

Beat.

NEUMANN *shakes ELENA's hand.*

ANNA. Do you remember Max Becker? He lived in our building. When I was little. We'd play hide and seek in the dark – and scare the life out of you.

NEUMANN *laughs.*

Don't you think Herr Neumann looks like him?

ELENA. Like Max Becker? No, not really.

NEUMANN *smiles.*

He was dark wasn't he?

ANNA. Fair, I think. No my mistake. Sorry.

The room reactivates – ELENA is ostracised.

HANS. Schwalbe 51? Isn't it? I've seen it in the car park outside the factory.

DIETER. You're handing out Schwalbes?

SCHMIDT. Neumann knows a guy.

DIETER. Course he does.

MARION *hits DIETER.*

What colour?

SCHMIDT. Grey. Come on. A man has to take himself seriously.

MARION. Do we need anything else?

DIETER. It's fine. Leave it.

MARION. I'm sure I brought some Erdnussflipps.

DIETER. Oh, go on then, I love a flip.

HANS *approaches.*

HANS. All okay?

ANNA. Yes – fine.

SOPHIE *and KARL chat at the window.*

HANS. Have you seen the new ones in blue?

SCHMIDT *doesn't pay attention.*

Who doesn't love a flip?

SCHMIDT. Christian – do you want a beer?

NEUMANN. Yes, that'd be great thanks.

HANS. **Shall we dance? Do you think we should get people dancing?**

ANNA *moves into the bedroom.*

Neumann – let's get you a beer. Who put this record on, it's appalling? Karl Wolf get your hands off my bloody record player.

BEDROOM

ANNA *frantically lights a cigarette, tries to catch her breath.*

34

NEUMANN TELLS HANS ABOUT ANNA

BEDROOM

ANNA *opens a window. Tries to catch her breath and gather herself.*

ANNA *smokes.*

SITTING ROOM

KARL *stops dancing with SOPHIE to try and get involved with NEUMANN and HANS.*

SOPHIE *is left standing.*

ELENA *keeps her eye on NEUMANN and HANS throughout.*

ELENA. How long have you been dating Karl?

SOPHIE. What? I haven't. God, no. No. No.

ELENA. Oh, my mistake. I'm sorry. Forgive me. *(Pause. Smiles knowingly.)* Won't be long though.

SOPHIE. No, I'm happy as I am for a while. My mother always said not to rush things.

ELENA. He's a kind lad, that counts for a lot.

KARL *comes over to* SOPHIE.

SITTING ROOM

DIETER. How long have you known Neumann?

SCHMIDT. Since we were teenagers.

MARION. Can you tell us anything we can use to embarrass him.

SCHMIDT. No, not really – he's always been pretty well behaved.

SITTING ROOM

NEUMANN *moves towards HANS – throws his arm around HANS, like they might be pals.*

NEUMANN *(whispered)*. Can I have a word?

HANS. Course.

NEUMANN. You should maybe check on your wife.

HANS. Anna? Check on her? Why? Where is she?

NEUMANN. I just introduced myself. She thought I was some chap from when she was younger, I felt bad for her, she seemed confused.

HANS *goes into the bedroom.*

ELENA. Karl, how nice you
could join us.

KARL *grabs* SOPHIE. ELENA
smiles. KARL *and* SOPHIE *dance.*

DIETER. You think you can get me a
Schwalbe if I'm well behaved?

THE RUSSIANS / BEDROOM

SITTING ROOM/KITCHEN

DIETER *and* ELENA *sit on the sofa.*

ELENA. Good to see you Dieter. How are things?

DIETER. Fine.

ELENA. You like the new boss?

DIETER. Come on, Elena. I can't.

ELENA. Of course.

DIETER. Robert was more fun, he had a sense of humour.

MARION. Karl!

ELENA (*to* MARION). I'll take them.

ELENA *comes to the hatch.*

MARION. Thank you. Keep them flat – (*Nibbles.*) will you. Come back – there's more.

SITTING ROOM

NEUMANN *stands alone –* SCHMIDT *beckons him over.*

SCHMIDT *lights* NEUMANN's *cigarette at the window.*

NEUMANN. You glad you came?

SCHMIDT. I'm not sure any of them are my type.

NEUMANN. The new secretary is good looking.

SCHMIDT. She's up for Karl.

NEUMANN. I'm still glad you came.

SCHMIDT. Yeah?

NEUMANN. I find these things awkward as hell. I never know how to speak to employees.

BEDROOM

HANS *enters.*

HANS. Hi love.

ANNA. Hi.

HANS. You going to join the party?

ANNA. His name is Max Becker. He was there when my mother died.

HANS. What do you mean?

ANNA. At the end of the war. When the Russians came, they killed my mother. Max helped them.

Pause.

HANS. You've always told me that your mother died in bombing.

ANNA. No.

HANS. Why didn't you tell me?

SITTING ROOM

SOPHIE *and* KARL *are looking at the records.*

KARL. Sophie, let me show you something. Right, so – where is it.

SOPHIE. Oh, wow – it's really old.

KARL. Yeah, it's cool though. He's got good stuff. Don't tell him.

SOPHIE. Can I pick one?

KARL. If you play one – put that one at the front.

SCHMIDT shoots a look at ELENA. ELENA nods gently, smiles.

MARION (shouting through, for a second platter). Can someone take these? Karl!

KARL. Leave me alone. I'm making magic happen.

SCHMIDT. Just have a good time.

NEUMANN. We'll go to the other party later, find you a lady.

SCHMIDT. We can stay as long as you need.

ELENA. Would either of you like some of these?

SCHMIDT. No thank you. SCHMIDT moves away.

NEUMANN. That's your house down there, no?

ELENA. Yes, how did you know that?

NEUMANN. Hans said. You're an old friend of the family?

ELENA smiles, nods slowly.

ELENA. What are you doing here?

NEUMANN. Excuse me?

ANNA. I was twelve. Russian soldiers were taking over the city. All the girls under sixteen had been hidden under the church, they'd told the Russians there was a cholera epidemic to keep them away. I'd stayed with my mother – I wouldn't leave her. She kept trying to make me go. We were hiding, I heard the soldiers at the bottom of the stairs. Their voices – their language – sounded loud and strange; shouting, laughing. They found Max in the lobby – asked him where we were. He showed them where we were hiding.

They burst in. My mother shielded me – they took her first. All three – (Beat.) she died. He stood next to me, Max, he stood and held my hand whilst we watched the whole thing.

SOPHIE plays with record player.

Oh, look he's got cards as well.

SOPHIE sits – KARL does a trick.

Choose a card. Can you imagine your card? I'm going to put them back in. Tap it three times. Is that your card?

KARL continues to do trick.

37

ELENA. Bosses don't tend to visit the houses of section managers.

NEUMANN. I'm new in town – these guys have been really welcoming. I was worried it looked weird, do you think it does?

ELENA (*beat*). No. I'm sure it's fine.

ELENA *looks away.*

SOPHIE *crosses to NEUMANN.*

NEUMANN. They were so friendly and honestly, I wanted the company. I brought Schmidt because I was nervous. Did Robert find that? That management was lonely?

ELENA. Oh look, I think someone wants to dance with you.

DIETER. Are we keeping you up?

SCHMIDT. Christian wants to go to some afterparty.

DIETER. Keeping his options open, is he?

SCHMIDT. Something like that.

DIETER. And what is it you do? You're a doctor, right?

SCHMIDT. You like your questions.

DIETER. You already know what I do.

SCHMIDT. Research. Humboldt.

DIETER. Intellectual? Eh?

SCHMIDT. We're all trying to break free of class oppression, Herr Bourmer.

HANS *holds ANNA whilst she sobs.*

HANS. I'm so sorry, my darling – you should have told me. (*Kissing and hugs.***)**

ANNA. That's Max Becker. In our sitting room, that man who is calling himself Christian Neumann, led those men to my mother.

HANS. I don't know what to do.

ANNA *stands up to leave.*

Where are you going?

ANNA. I'm going to ask him to leave.

HANS. You can't do that.

ANNA. Why not?

HANS. He's a Party member. I'd lose my job. We'd be arrested.

ANNA. He told my mother's murderers where to find her.

MARION *shouts.*

SOPHIE. No way. That's amazing. How did you do that?

SOPHIE *goes to buffet to dance.*

I should go and help Marion.

SOPHIE *crosses to NEUMANN.*

DIETER. Any news on those meatballs Marion?

NEUMANN. Did someone say meatballs?

DIETER *and* NEUMANN *laugh.*

MARION intercepts DIETER.
She kisses him on the cheek.

DIETER. You're brilliant, you know that.

MARION. Stop winding people up, come and help me.

DIETER goes to the hatch, to help MARION – he finds a bag of pretzels on the side.

DIETER. Karl! Go long!

DIETER holds the bag up like he's going to throw it. KARL moves – with SOPHIE – to catch it. DIETER throws it – it hits the front window hard –

ELENA arranges for NEUMANN and SOPHIE to dance. They're not entirely willing.

NEUMANN. Honestly, no – no – ask Schmidt. I really can't though. I'm not good.

They spin awkwardly – NEUMANN's not very good – he's nervous and a bit clumsy.

SOPHIE. Are you okay?

NEUMANN. I hate dancing, I don't understand anyone that can do it without making an idiot of themselves.

SOPHIE. It's fine, you just have to imagine that no one is watching.

NEUMANN. But they are – they're all watching.

SOPHIE. Just keep your eyes on me.

ANNA opens the door. HANS closes it.

HANS. He says he doesn't know who Max Becker is.

ANNA. Hans?

HANS. It was twenty years ago.

ANNA. He's been following me.

HANS. What?

ANNA. He stepped onto the U-Bahn, months ago. I knew it was him, he hasn't changed. I could feel it. The shape of him, is exactly the same as when we were young. The shape of him.

HANS. You might be confused.

ANNA. I'm not confused. It's him.

HANS. He says he has no idea. Elena says she doesn't recognise him. He's a good guy.

MARION. Hold your horses lads, you don't want to eat them raw. They're coming. Can someone take these in the meantime?

No one does – MARION offers nibbles.

39

KARL *launches himself to get it.*

ELENA. Careful!

MARION. Don't do that!

KARL *misses the bag of pretzels. The pretzels hit the front wall and explode. KARL bashes ELENA by mistake. NEUMANN leaps to her defence, catches her.*

NEUMANN. Oi! Karl, watch what you're doing. Karl! Come on.

NEUMANN, KARL, SOPHIE *deal with the pretzels and laugh. People recover from the wreckage and notice…*

NEUMANN. Honestly, I'm fine.

NEUMANN *stands centre – smokes at the front window.*

People in the sitting room react.

HANS. I've got to change my shirt.

HANS *changes his shirt.*

You haven't been sleeping. You're tired.

ANNA (*shouting*). HANS!

I can feel him in the room even when I can't see him. I can feel him. He's here for me.

HANS. He's here because we invited him.

ANNA. He told you to have a party in the flat that he has given us, to celebrate the promotion that he has given you. He's done it all to get to me.

HANS. I've worked so hard for all this, I've spent years celebrating your success – and this is the first thing /

ANNA. / Hans?

...HANS and his flamboyant shirt. The room bursts into laughter celebration/mockery – HANS looks overwhelmed by it – he doesn't know what to do. The music is loud.

NEUMANN. I like it – I think it's a brilliant shirt, leave the man alone.

NEUMANN starts to dance, he makes himself look silly – in empathy with HANS. The two men make themselves look daft, it's endearing.

Cossack dance.

DIETER. That's the ugliest shirt I've ever seen.

SOPHIE. It's so modern though!

MARION looks through and laughs.

ELENA. I think it's lovely.

DIETER. He's a section manager these days.

MARION. Don't be unkind. It's a great shirt Hans!

NEUMANN laughs and joins him in his dance. SCHMIDT laughs.

KARL. Where did you get it?

HANS. The Exquisite.

HANS. We've got guests.

HANS exits.

DIETER sticks his head in.

DIETER. Anna? You okay?

ANNA. I'm fine. Yes. Why? Just finding my lipstick.

DIETER. That's not lipstick, that's a cigarette, darling. Come on – come and join the party.

ANNA. Just coming.

SCHMIDT. On the sausage and meat counter?

HANS. Come on – it's not that bad. I like it. I'm fine with it.

DIETER *takes the second platter from* MARION. HANS *nearly sends it flying.*

DIETER. Whoa! Whoa! Whoa!

NEUMANN *goes to the table and picks up a bottle of Rötkappchen. He shakes it provocatively.*

SCHMIDT. Christian!

SOPHIE. No! No! Don't. Sorry but.

KARL. Oh my god, great – go on! Do it!

MARION. If that goes all over the floor. It won't be you clearing it up.

HANS. If that goes on the carpet, Anna will /

MARION. / I know.

HANS *back into the sitting room.*

HANS. Please don't get it on the carpets – guys? Please!

KARL. Go on! Do it! Do it!

SCHMIDT. Christian. Christian!

NEUMANN. Come on, everyone round – let's celebrate – come on! It'll be fun.

NEUMANN *giggles, nervous –* SCHMIDT *rolls his eyes,* NEUMANN *threatens to open the bottle.*

CRESCENDO

ANNA *enters the sitting room.*

The bottle pops, the fizz goes everywhere, the crowd screams, whoops, and cheers and laughs – the sound is overwhelming, cacophonous.

MARION *goes into the kitchen to get a cloth to mop up the fizz.*

ANNA. Hans? Hans?

HANS *(shouting over to* ANNA *from where he is).* It's okay! It's not on the carpet! I promise I got nothing on the carpets, I promise!

NEUMANN. One to everyone.

SOPHIE *grabs the cheese hedgehog, to stop it from being drowned by the fizz.*

Grab some glasses!

KARL. Where are the glasses? Hans?

HANS *points to the dresser.*

MARION *comes careering out of the kitchen with a towel, to clean up.* SOPHIE *runs towards the kitchen (with hedgehog) yelping.* SOPHIE *bumps into* MARION, *the cheese hedgehog goes everywhere.* SOPHIE *dives onto the floor to try and pick it up.* ANNA *nearly trips over* SOPHIE. MARION *does trip over* SOPHIE. ANNA, *just, steps out of the way of it.*

NEUMANN. Are you okay? Sophie – are you alright?

MARION *mops up.* ELENA *helps.* SOPHIE *collects herself.* ANNA *moves out of the madness.*

HANS. Anna?

43

ANNA. Yes?

HANS. Are you –

ANNA. Going to try and have fun? Sure. It's a party.

ANNA moves away from HANS.

NEUMANN. Frau Weber.

ANNA. It's Anna.

NEUMANN. Can I get you a drink? It's Rötkappchen, or a beer –

ANNA. I'm fine thank you. I'm going to get some water.

NEUMANN hands her a drink.

NEUMANN. Look, here we go. It's a lovely apartment. It's kind of you to have us all here.

ANNA. It's my pleasure.

ANNA *moves away into KARL and SCHMIDT.*

KARL. I know you from somewhere – don't I?

SCHMIDT. I don't think so.

KARL. I do. KJS sports school. You were our medic.

DIETER. Fill me up, I'm driving.

SCHMIDT. Where do you live?

DIETER *(in response).* A tiny place in Grünau.

KARL. They've got gnomes.

DIETER *and HANS grab glasses and try to catch the champagne as fast as it's coming out of the bottle. They hand out the glasses.*

SOPHIE. I'm sorry, I'm so sorry. I just, I just,

MARION. It's okay.

SOPHIE. I just saw the explosion coming.

MARION. It's fine.

NEUMANN. One to everyone – I want everyone to have a glass.

SOPHIE. Oh god, what if it stains, I'm so sorry.

ANNA. I didn't know you were at sports school, Karl?

KARL. Yeah, big star.

ANNA. What happened /

SCHMIDT *moves away.*

KARL. Schmidt?

ANNA *watches* NEUMANN *and* HANS *chatting – laughing.*

MARION (*from the floor*). They're not gnomes! They're ornaments.

DIETER. What was that about?

KARL. Nothing.

DIETER. Where do you know him from?

KARL. Sports school.

DIETER. How?

KARL. Leave it.

MARION. It wasn't you that shook the bloody bottle everywhere.

SOPHIE. I'm so sorry.

HANS. It's fine, please – both of you, don't worry.

MARION. Sophie, really – please. Stop apologising. It's aggravating.

MARION *moves into the kitchen with the dirty rags.*

45

KITCHEN – PRE-TOAST

HALLWAY	KITCHEN	SITTING ROOM	SITTING ROOM
ANNA *runs to the front door –* *she sees it and thinks about going out of it.*		NEUMANN. Hans, can I have a word? Thought we'd do a little toast.	DIETER. Is that sparkles? On that top – is that what you'd call that?
SCHMIDT. Frau Weber?		HANS. Yes, that's a great idea. What do we need to organise?	SOPHIE. I guess so.
ANNA. Yes.		NEUMANN. Is there a problem?	
ANNA *turns to* SCHMIDT, *stares at him.*		HANS. With the toast? There shouldn't be.	DIETER. There isn't another word for it? What is that?
SCHMIDT. Are you leaving?		NEUMANN. With your wife?	
ANNA. No, I was just – only a walk. I.	*Meatball sizzle/splash.*	HANS. I think she's fine. She's just /	SOPHIE. I don't know, I think it's just a shape. My
SCHMIDT. Are you feeling okay?		NEUMANN. / I'm sorry – if I – I'm just worried I haven't helped.	
ANNA. No. I think I'm unwell.	MARION. Oh no, the meatballs are burnt.	*Beat.*	
MARION *enters with the debris from the hedgehog.* ANNA *follows her into the kitchen.*	ANNA. Don't throw them – we'll serve them later.	HANS. I think she's fine. Why don't we get this toast organised? Not to blow my own trumpet. We should just get /	
SCHMIDT *stands in the hall – gets something from his coat – puts it in his pocket.* KARL *enters.*	ANNA *pours herself a large glass of water and glugs it down, she can hardly breathe.*	ELENA. / How are you doing?	

KARL. We're meant to get glasses, aren't we?

SCHMIDT. For sure.

Pause – KARL stares at SCHMIDT.

KARL. You don't remember me?

SCHMIDT. I don't think I do.

KARL. Karl Wolf – I was a thrower.

SCHMIDT. Hm.

KARL. Started on track but they moved me on to javelin.

SCHMIDT. I'm sorry, I /

KARL. / You don't remember working at the school – or you don't remember me?

SCHMIDT. Could I get past?

KARL. We used to have meetings with you once a week.

HANS *is signalling at her.*

MARION. It's killed Dieter, Hans getting this promotion.

ANNA. Why?

MARION. He feels like everyone is younger than him and doing better than him.

ANNA *watches* HANS *and* NEUMANN. MARION *watches* DIETER *and* SOPHIE.

Look at him with Sophie. It used to make him sick, watching men acting like that with me. Now he's doing it. It's awful, it's like he feels he's missed out on something and he wants to get it back. (*Shakes her head.*)

ANNA *watches.*

ANNA. That's life, no?

MARION. Is it?

ANNA. It's disappointing.

HANS. I think we're thinking about getting some glasses together, so we can do a toast.

NEUMANN. Do you think you could help us with that? Trying to get everybody organised?

ELENA. Of course.

NEUMANN. That would be great. Thank you.

ELENA *exits.*

I didn't realise you knew the Hillenbrands so well.

HANS. Um. She used to be our neighbour.

NEUMANN. That can't have been fun – living next door to the boss.

HANS. He's a – generally, he was a – I mean – he was – a good guy, we're old friends.

NEUMANN. From work?

mother got it for me for my birthday.

DIETER. She sounds like she's a nice lady.

SOPHIE. I like things that have pattern, she says I'm a magpie.

DIETER. You don't look a thing like one.

SOPHIE. No, not that I look like one but because I like sparkly things.

DIETER. I know. I was joking.

HANS. Good one, Dieter.

SCHMIDT. It's not an admirable quality to be quite so insistent, I've made it clear that /

KARL. / You prick.

SCHMIDT. Excuse me?

KARL. I could have been /

SCHMIDT. / But it didn't work out, did it?

KARL. It wasn't my fault. You used to give us a white powder.

ANNA. Karl?

SCHMIDT. Herr Wolf.

KARL. We were kids. You know what that stuff did?

ANNA swoops in and grabs KARL – she drags him into the sitting room.

ANNA. Don't do that, Karl. Come on.

MARION. **Are you okay? You're shaking.**

ANNA. **I'm tired.**

MARION. **Anna?**

ANNA. **I keep seeing people that aren't there.**

MARION. **What?**

ANNA. **They're doing the toast, we should go.**

MARION exits. ANNA steps into the alcove where she can hear SCHMIDT and KARL, they can't see her. She listens.

HANS. Elena knew Anna when she was younger.

NEUMANN. How so?

HANS. They lived in the same building. Um. I think Elena was friends with Anna's mother?

NEUMANN. Are they still friends?

HANS. Who?

NEUMANN. Elena and Anna's mother.

HANS. No.

NEUMANN. That seems like a shame.

HANS. Anna's mother is dead. She died in the war.

NEUMANN. That makes sense.

HANS. What do you mean?

NEUMANN. That she'd want to keep Elena in her life. It's difficult as a – obviously – but if they're old friends.

SOPHIE. Sorry, I didn't realise you were making a joke.

DIETER (*shouting*). It's fine, it wasn't a very good one.

KARL. I could have been /

ANNA. / I know. I know. Let's go through for the toast. Let's toast Hans. He's done really well.

KARL (*quiet – as she takes him through*). Thanks.

MARION *whispers to DIETER what ANNA has just told her. DIETER looks for ANNA, concerned.*

ANNA (*whispered*). Karl knows Schmidt.

ELENA (*whispered*). Years ago.

HANS. Yes.

NEUMANN. It's important we keep our teachers feeling good. They're the future of our country.

HANS. Yes.

NEUMANN *turns to the hatch.*

NEUMANN. Everyone grab a drink.

MARION *enters the sitting room.*

SOPHIE (*to MARION*). I just wanted to save the hedgehog. It's so silly, it's doesn't even matter. It's just a stupid hedgehog. I don't even know why I thought it mattered, I /

MARION. / Shut up, Sophie – please.

DIETER. It's a party.

ELENA. But we can hardly hear ourselves think.

MARION *stands, already exhausted. DIETER throws his arm round her – puts a kiss on her cheek.*

DIETER. Maz. Come on. Join in. (*About SOPHIE.*) You seen that skirt? She's wearing a couple of threads.

They fill the final few glasses.

NEUMANN *puts an awful lot into SOPHIE's glass.*

DIETER. Anna okay?

HANS. Mm. She's fine.

SOPHIE. No, no – please don't.

NEUMANN. No party poopers allowed.

ELENA *goes to the record player to turn down the music.*

NEUMANN. Frau Weber, Anna? Can I fill you up?

ANNA. Thank you – that's kind.

NEUMANN. No trouble at all.

HANS (*grabs ANNA and pulls her to him*). Okay?

NEUMANN. Let's do a toast – everyone round here, I want them all filled nice and high – Hans? Has everyone got a drink?

ANNA *looks up at HANS. She's miles away. He kisses her. Tries to reassure her. ANNA whimpers slightly under her breath.*

Come on, everybody, come on.

KARL *is still filling SOPHIE's glass.*

SOPHIE's *glass is filled right up.*

SOPHIE. No, stop – please.

NEUMANN. Come on!

SOPHIE (*whispered*). Oh god.

THE TOAST

NEUMANN *turns on* SOPHIE, *aggressively.*

NEUMANN. What did you just say?

SOPHIE. I said /

NEUMANN. / Sophie, I asked what you just said.

SOPHIE. I –

NEUMANN. Was that dissent? Did anyone else just hear dissent?

SOPHIE. I said. 'Oh god'.

SOPHIE can't speak. NEUMANN *glares. Beat. Then – bursts into laughter, throws his arm round* SOPHIE.

NEUMANN *(laughs)*. I'm joking! I'm joking. (*Close in to* SOPHIE.) I'm joking, I promise. Oh god, your face, I'm sorry – It was only a joke, I swear, I didn't mean to worry you. It was a joke. Sorry, that was a bad joke. I'm sorry. It was just a joke.

The room half-laughs – tries to relax.

Record crackles under the speech.

In these past few weeks, where I have been delighted, I mean – all of you, delighted – (*Playfully pokes at* HANS.) to have had the privilege of being your new works manager. I have noted the diligence, dedication and attention to detail of every single one of you, you are not only good workers, and good citizens – but good socialists… /

ELENA. / Bravo!

NEUMANN. …comrades this country can be proud of. Hans Weber has been at Industriewerke Ludwigsfelde for ten years and, as far as I can see, he works every day like it's his first. This apartment – this couple are a perfect example of what

51

we could all be. What we should want to be and can be. There is no one more deserving of the position of section manager! Three cheers for Hans Weber!

CROWD. Hoch! Hoch! Hoch!

DIETER *burps*.

MARION. Dieter, that's disgusting!

NEUMANN. When is the little one going to arrive? Everyone is thinking it. (*Awkward laughter.*) Give her a kiss! Go on – give her a kiss!

CROWD. Give her a kiss!

HANS *and* ANNA *kiss – more cheering*.

HANS. I'd just like to say – (*Glasses still in the air.*) none of it would mean anything without this brilliant woman. She has stood by me, supported me – given me a home to come home to and a real desire to be the best man I can.

HANS *kisses the top of her head.* ANNA *manages a smile. They knock their drink back – stamp, cheer and whoop –* SOPHIE *looks like she's going to puke.*

DIETER *burps.*

ANNA *starts to climb up onto the sideboard.*

THE SPEECH

ANNA *steps up onto the table.*

HANS. Anna, love? What are you doing?

DIETER. What's she doing?

MARION. She said she was feeling weird.

NEUMANN *stares.*

ANNA. I just want to get up here. I just want to stand up where I can /

HANS. / Come down. Come down – love.

ANNA. Get off.

ELENA. Anna, the fireworks are on soon – why don't we go up and watch the fireworks?

HANS. Anna, get down love. Please – love – get down – what are you doing?

NEUMANN. Hans?

HANS. I think she's – it's a joke – probably – she's just feeling a bit /

ANNA *stands on a chair. She seems unsteady – but the second she starts speaking – she rises to strength, stride and force of conviction.*

ANNA. / 'Something new has happened. People of the DDR. Something new.

HANS. Anna?

ANNA. For the first time in German history – our fatherland is guided by a plan that considers only the needs of the people.' This is what I say to my class. Can you imagine – I say to the students – use your imagination to dream – see in your dreams, a country where every citizen works together –

53

DIETER. Anna, get down.

ANNA. WILL YOU JUST BACK OFF!

DIETER. Oi!

ANNA. I'm trying to say something. I'm trying to get something *said.*

HANS crosses to make a phone call – ANNA, distracted by it, tries to continue.

A whole people that go to their work and tend to their homes – with the heat and pride and purpose of a common endeavour, to make our country good –

HANS picks up the telephone.

Imagine that? Who are you calling, Hans? Hans? (*To the crowd.*) Imagine – all of you – a people that are not made miserable by a hunger for profit, a people that are not made fearful by systems that fail them, not made anxious by comparisons they can never win.

Imagine a people for whom their country feels like family, support and community – no longer deep sickness of inequality. Imagine this land – I say to the students. Imagine this land – because this is where we live! (*Takes a breath, we can hear the blood in her ears, her heart pumping, hard, with a dream.*) The future belongs to socialism!

ANNA wobbles on the chair.

HANS (*telephone*). Fred. It's Hans – Yeah, fine. I'm glad you're in actually – I uh. Do you think you could pop over? It's Anna. Yes. Fine. Just – she's – a bit. I don't know, if you're free just – could you – Thanks. Great. I'd be really grateful. Thanks.

HANS puts down the phone.

NEUMANN (*with respect*). Glück und Friede sei beschieden Deutschland. Deutsche Demokratische Republik – einig Vaterland!

PARTY (*inc.* HANS). Deutsche Demokratische Republik – einig Vaterland!

Everyone does the toast.

ANNA *stands, stares at* HANS.

ANNA *kicks the chair over.*

HANS *stands on the opposite side of the room, he can't move.*

NEUMANN *goes over to* ANNA.

NEUMANN (*kindly*). Lovely speech, Frau Weber.

ANNA. It's Anna.

NEUMANN. Shall we help you down? Karl?

He lifts her off the chair.

ANNA (*to* DIETER). Why are you looking at me like that?

DIETER. I'm worried about you.

ANNA (*shouting*). Who were you calling, Hans?

DIETER (*grabbing her*). What are you doing?

ANNA. Me? I'm not the one trying to fuck twenty-year-olds that can barely spell their own name.

MARION. Stop.

ANNA. Just because my husband's promotion has made you feel injured. She doesn't fancy you – she's giving you time because she feels beholden to men of your age, that's all.

55

MARION. I said /

ANNA. / I should be quiet and scurry around making sure all the little bits of food are on all the right little bitty plates so that everyone can have a lovely time?

DIETER. Anna.

ANNA. You pick up after every one of this lot every single day of your life and they never once say thank you.

Fireworks.

SOPHIE. Look, the fireworks have started. I love fireworks.

ANNA. Of course, you do.

ANNA *takes* SOPHIE'*s face in her hands.*

You're so new. You should go up to the roof and watch the fireworks, the view is amazing.

HANS (*to the room, trying to normalise*). We went up at New Year. You can see all the way down to Alexanderplatz.

SCHMIDT (*whispered to* NEUMANN). I've got something I could give her to help her calm down.

ELENA (*to the room*). Shall we give Anna some space. Hm? Who was on the phone?

NEUMANN (*aside*). Let's speak to Hans. Hans?

HANS (*to* ELENA). A friend of Anna's.

HANS *is pulled over to where* NEUMANN *is standing.*

ELENA. Who?

ANNA. Where's the cake? I made a cake for Hans – where is that cake I made /

MARION. / I made the cake. You didn't make it.

ANNA (*shouting*). I STAYED UP ALL NIGHT MAKING A CAKE.

HANS. Okay everybody, why don't we all go up on the roof and watch the fireworks? We can get some fresh air and then come back down for /

/ NEUMANN *whispers in HANS's ear whilst he's talking.*

NEUMANN. Hans?

HANS. I'm sorry, I –

ANNA. Why is everyone always saying things that no one else is allowed to hear?

NEUMANN. Who were you calling?

ELENA. We're going up to the roof. Do you want to lie down?

SCHMIDT. I just wondered if I could help?

ANNA. Are you going to try and make me quiet, like everyone made you quiet?

HANS. Help?

NEUMANN. Who was the friend?

The room goes silent – turns on ANNA.

The same way no one will talk to Elena? (*Loud whisper.*) Because no one will mention that Robert got carted off in the middle of the afternoon – and that's he's probably dead. She found his glasses smashed, and he can't see further than the end of his arm without those glasses. (*Pause.*) But no one will talk about it even though he was a good and kind and loyal boss to you all for decades. It's not very good of you, comrades. It's not very good of you at all. Instead you all swear allegiance to the new guy in a *flash.*

ANNA *collapses onto the sofa.*

MARION. Darling, you're not feeling well.

SCHMIDT. Let me help.

DIETER. She's okay.

NEUMANN. Is she?

DIETER. She doesn't need /

57

HANS. / Dieter – it's not really your /

DIETER. I lived through the war; we didn't just hand out tablets when someone was a bit overwrought.

ELENA. No, we let them blow their brains out instead.

NEUMANN. I think Frau Hillenbrand should leave.

Pause. The room goes silent.

HANS approaches ELENA.

ELENA. I'm suddenly very tired. I'll call you when I get home.

ELENA exits.

DIETER (*whispered to* ANNA). Please tell me what's going on.

SOPHIE (*to* KARL). Help her. You should help her.

KARL (*muttered*). Don't take anything that guy gives you.

NEUMANN. Dieter. Karl.

MARION. Karl, Dieter – your coats.

KARL and DIETER stand a moment, they look like they won't move.

Beat. KARL and DIETER head for the door with MARION and SOPHIE.

DIETER (*whispered*). What did you tell her?

KARL. I can't watch this.

SOPHIE. Shall I get her coats.

KARL and SOPHIE leave.

MARION. Nothing.

DIETER (*whispered*). What did you say?

NEUMANN. Anna, this is Dr Schmidt. He's an old friend of mine from university. I've known him a really long time.

ANNA takes the tablets, swallows them down with water.

MARION. Just come on, leave them to it.

MARION *and* DIETER *leave.*

ANNA. Now I can just have a sleep.

HANS. Now you can just have a sleep.

Fireworks.

I can hear them exploding, can you hear them exploding? I feel like I can hear the explosions.

NEUMANN. It's just the fireworks Frau Weber. They're really beautiful, look.

ANNA (*looking out the front window*). How can anyone in this city blow things up for fun and call it beautiful?

NEUMANN. Schmidt, will you make sure Elena gets back to her house?

Beat – silence – something threatening.

SCHMIDT. Yes. (*To ANNA.*) I hope you feel better, Frau Weber.

ANNA *nods.*

NEUMANN (*quietly to* SCHMIDT). I'll be on the roof when you get back.

SCHMIDT *exits.* NEUMANN, HANS *and* ANNA *are left alone.*

I'll see you up there, Hans?

HANS. Sure.

NEUMANN. Rest well, Frau Weber.

ANNA. I'm sorry for all the fuss.

59

NEUMANN. You're fine. Just get well.

    NEUMANN exits.

HANS. I'll stay.

ANNA. I'd rather be alone. Really.

    ANNA staggers slightly.

HANS. Let me help you to bed. You've had a shock.

ANNA (*looks at* HANS). I have.

HANS. My darling, my love – I only think that you're confused. That's all and I'm worried for you. I'll turn the lights off.

    HANS goes into the bedroom.

FRED

FRED. Hello.

FRED *enters*.

Hello? Anna?

ANNA. Fred.

FRED. Are you alright? Hans rang and asked me to come down.

ANNA. Why?

FRED. What's going on? Where's the party?

HANS *comes back in*.

HANS. I thought she might be better at comforting you. I thought it might be better if you had a friend.

ANNA. I'm fine.

FRED. What's happened?

HANS. My new boss, Anna has him confused for a childhood friend.

ANNA. I thought I recognised him from when my mum died. The boy that was there when /

FRED. / Oh god. Anna. Are you okay?

HANS. You knew about this?

FRED. Yes.

ANNA. It's not something people talk about.

61

FRED. Is it the same boy?

Pause.

ANNA. No. Honestly. It's not him. I don't think it's him.

FRED. You're sure?

ANNA. For some reason all that stuff, today – just came back, I don't know why – seeing him – I just, I was sure it was him. But – it's not – I don't know what – anyway. It's all fine. It's fine – you should go and /

/ NEUMANN *enters.*

NEUMANN. Hans? I can't find the door up to the /

/ FRED *makes a noise of shock.*

ANNA. What?

NEUMANN. Hi.

HANS. Christian? This is –

NEUMANN. Fred.

FRED. What are you doing here? I'm in my work clothes.

NEUMANN. Hans and Anna had a party for Hans's promotion – I was invited.

FRED. I live upstairs.

NEUMANN. I know. I've been there.

FRED. Sorry, yes – um.

NEUMANN. I didn't realise it was the same place until I got here, I was going to maybe knock later /

FRED. / This is Christian, the guy I mentioned /

NEUMANN. / I'm her new boyfriend, is it okay to say that?

FRED. Yes, that's okay. It's nice.

Flirt. Smiles. They're into each other. Beat.

ANNA. Where did you meet?

FRED. In Bar Moskau. Few weekends ago.

NEUMANN. Three months.

FRED. Stop it.

NEUMANN. I'm glad you're here.

FRED. It's good to see you. Anna, are you okay?

FRED moves to ANNA. HANS and NEUMANN chat.

ANNA. Christian is who I confused for the boy that /

FRED. / But what was his name? The boy was called Max, wasn't he?

ANNA. Yes, they just look so similar.

FRED. Christian's from Leipzig.

ANNA. Is he?

FRED. I've met his sister.

ANNA. Oh?

63

64

FRED. She's lovely.

ANNA. I just got confused. I'm sorry.

NEUMANN. Don't be sorry.

ANNA. All of you, honestly – I'm fine, I'm so sorry this has been, I'm tired I think – that's all. You lot go up – I'll just rest for a second.

FRED. I should stay.

ANNA. No, really – just give me a couple of minutes alone and I'll be better. Can you turn the lights off? It's too bright.

HANS *puts his arm round* ANNA.

NEUMANN. You want to come up?

FRED. I'm not ready.

NEUMANN. You look amazing.

FRED *joins* ANNA *on the sofa.*

FRED. I guess I could grab my coat.

NEUMANN (*to* HANS). Shall we take a bottle? Stay warm.

FRED. He's great. You'll like him.

HANS. Good idea.

ANNA *nods.*

NEUMANN *opens a bottle.*

NEUMANN. You sure we can't convince you Frau Weber?

ANNA. Go and have fun.

ANNA *walks* FRED *to the door.*

ANNA. No really, I'll stay.

HANS *kisses* ANNA *on the cheek.*

FRED. I'll see you on the roof.

FRED *exits.*

NEUMANN. I'm sorry it's been /

ANNA. / Oh god no, it's me that should be saying sorry. It's my husband's promotion and I've caused such a scene. I've ruined it.

NEUMANN. It's fine, you're fine. No one minds.

NEUMANN *kisses ANNA goodbye.*

(*Whispered.*) I'm never going to let you go.

NEUMANN *exits.*

ANNA *by the door.* HANS *takes her face in his hands.*

HANS. You're going to be okay. Get some sleep and it will all be okay.

THE DISAPPEARANCE OF HANS

HANS *turns off the lights because ANNA is sleepy.*

ANNA. I could have told you you were good at your job if it mattered that much.

HANS. What?

Smash. Lights out.

What the hell was that? Someone's smashed the light in the corridor.

HANS *goes to the corridor.*

ANNA. Hans?

HANS *(from the corridor)*. It isn't working.

ANNA. What can you see? Hans? Hans?

HANS *doesn't respond.*

ANNA *tries the main switch.*

Hans? Hans? The fuse has blown – Hans? Where have you gone? Hans?

The phone rings.

ANNA *goes to pick the phone up – as she does so, the phone stops ringing.*

Total darkness.

ANNA *stands in the doorway.*

Hans? (*Weakly.*) Hans – the fuse has blown. (*Swallows.*) I don't want to come out there in the dark. I'm going to get a torch.

ANNA *can hear a distant coughing.*

Hans? Are you there? Hans!

ANNA *heads into the kitchen – she opens all the drawers – she's looking for a torch. She can't find one.*

NOT ALONE / MAX AND ANNA

ANNA *breathes, heavily.*

ANNA *heads to the cupboard that we know has the matches in it.*

ANNA *stumbles over some bottles.*

ANNA *crashes into them.*

ANNA. Fuck. Ow. Ow – *(Inhales sharply in pain.)* Shit. Ow. It's bleeding. Tchh.

A music box with 'Der Mond ist aufgegangen' … starts to play in the bedroom.

Hello? Is anyone there?

ANNA *goes into the bedroom.*

ANNA *approaches the music box – it snaps shut.*

Hello?

The sound of a human moving in the dark.

ANNA *comes back into the living room.*

Hello? Is anyone in here.

The front door slams.

Hans, Hans – Hans? Is that you?

A bottle spins near the sideboard.

ANNA *goes to get the torch from out of the sideboard.*

ANNA *reveals* NEUMANN's *face in the light.*

ANNA *drops the torch.*

ANNA *breathes deeply.*

NEUMANN *lights his Zippo lighter.*

NEUMANN *lights a candle.*

You've got a candle.

MAX. It's like when we used to hide in the basement during air raids.

ANNA. How did you know the lights would go out?

MAX. Because I turned them out. You're not bleeding. You said you were bleeding.

ANNA. My husband –

MAX. Hans, his name is Hans – have you forgotten your own husband's name?

ANNA. Where is he?

MAX. He's gone down to the basement to check the fuse box. It will take him a while. (*Holds the candle to her face.*) You look so much the same.

ANNA *backs up.*

ANNA. You've been following me.

MAX. And two or three times you've stopped and looked back and smiled.

ANNA *stumbles.*

69

Careful, those pills are strong – especially if you've had a drink.

ANNA. You shouldn't exploit your position as a Party member for personal gain.

MAX. When we saw each other on the U-Bahn, the first time in twenty-three years, when we looked at each other – we both – what we felt.

Beat – ANNA breaks away.

ANNA. How did you get a job at my husband's factory? What have you done to Robert?

MAX. They just offered me the job. I don't know where Robert has gone, I promise I don't know.

ANNA. I don't believe you.

MAX. It's not until I saw your picture on Hans' desk that I knew he was your husband.

ANNA. He's going to be back in a minute.

MAX. I come back to the city and I'm asked to manage your husband's factory. It's a sign.

ANNA laughs. Breathes.

ANNA. You believe in signs? I live with my husband. I love my husband.

MAX. He left you here alone when you weren't feeling well.

ANNA. I asked him to go.

MAX. You told him who I was – what I'd done – and he defended his job before believing you.

ANNA. You're his manager.

MAX. You're his wife.

ANNA. It's individualistic to be loyal to your partner before the state.

MAX. Two people don't need anyone else if they're the right two people.

ANNA. Do you know how quickly that sort of self-involvement makes a society dissolve?

MAX. You're just not really in love with your husband.

MAX *blows out the candle and kisses ANNA. She lets him then breaks off.*

ANNA. That's not love. Love makes me happy. That's – ego. It makes, it'll destroy you.

MAX. Tell me you haven't spent years wondering where I am.

ANNA. I love my husband. I love our life.

MAX. But do you want your husband?

ANNA. You can't build a country on want.

MAX. Your Party leaders are all want – they're living like kings in Wandlitz – they want for nothing whilst the rest of the country queue for food.

ANNA. Was that dissent? Did anyone else just hear dissent?

NEUMANN *comes close – close enough to kiss her.*

MAX. I've missed you.

ANNA *stops him.*

–

Do you remember when you couldn't sleep? And you'd tap on my bedroom wall and I'd crouch next to the bit where your bed was on the other side and I'd sing – and you'd sing back –

71

He sings 'Der Monde ist aufgegangen' – after a little while, she joins in with him.

And when you stopped, I know you'd gone all peaceful and sleepy.

ANNA *nods a little – she's tired.* NEUMANN *strokes her face.*

ANNA. You look just like you did when you were a little boy. (*Beat.*) When the Russian soldiers asked you whether were there any women in the house, why didn't you just say no?

Beat.

Instead – you led them to us. Why?

Beat.

We'd known each other since we were born. You were my best friend. You promised you'd keep us safe.

MAX. Stop it.

ANNA. I loved you.

MAX. Stop.

ANNA. You led them to us. They killed my mother.

MAX. They didn't touch you. They left you alone. I gave them your mother to keep you safe.

ANNA. That's bullshit. They left because they were spent.

MAX. And after we cleared up the blood and you took my hand and you led me into the bedroom and you made me lie on the bed and you said we were like husband and wife and this was the honeymoon suite and you got on top of me and when I said stop you laughed and said, 'boys don't say stop' and you carried on.

ANNA. Why did you show them where we were?

MAX. We'd never even kissed, we promised we'd keep each other safe, we were good – and you ruined us.

ANNA. All you had to say was that the building was empty!

MAX. They said if I showed them where people were, they'd give me cigarettes.

ANNA. Is that it?

MAX. I was fourteen. I'm sorry.

–

ANNA. I was twelve. I'm sorry.

ANNA kisses him. MAX kisses her back – it's gentle – it's forgiveness.

The lights come back on.

He's fixed it. He's coming back up.

MAX rushes to get the record.

What are you doing?

MAX. Come with me.

ANNA. Come with you where?

MAX organises the record/headphones.

Come with you, where?

MAX. Why don't you have children?

Beat.

73

74

MAX *gives ANNA passports from his inside pocket. ANNA looks at them. MAX keeps doing the headphones.*

These are American passports.

ANNA *tries not to take them – to hand them back, MAX resists – they're dangerous.*

How have you got my picture? (*Desperately tries to give them back to him.*) **I don't want them. Take them away!**

MAX. **We'll drive to the American checkpoint. We'll go across tonight.**

ANNA. **We'll be shot.**

MAX. **My friends will make sure we're safe. There's a flight for us in the morning.**

ANNA *backs away from him.*

ANNA. **Friends? American friends? What have you done?**

MAX. **You'll love it there. I promise. You're allowed to be new.**

MAX *puts headphones on ANNA.*

ANNA. **What are you doing?**

MAX *plays ANNA 'California Dreamin'' by The Mamas and the Papas.*

ANNA *kisses MAX.*

HANS INTERRUPTS / THE ENDING

HANS *unlocks the door and enters.*

HANS. I had to go down to the fuse /

/ ANNA *stops kissing* MAX. *The space between them isn't big enough for* HANS *not to suspect something.* ANNA, *in a panic, runs towards* HANS – *the earphone cord goes taught –* NEUMANN *tries to grab it – but it pulls the headphone jack out of the record player – 'California Dreamin'' blasts out of the record player.* HANS *stands, shocked – not sure what to do.*

Anna?

NEUMANN. Does this belong to you?

HANS. The record? No – I've never heard it before. What was going on when I came in?

NEUMANN *takes the record off the stereo.*

FRED *enters.*

FRED. Hans? Where did you go?

HANS. I was fixing the fuse. Anna?

NEUMANN. Do you understand the implications of a newly appointed section manager having an American record in his apartment?

FRED. Oi, I thought you were coming up to the roof?

HANS. I've never seen it before. I don't know how it got in here.

FRED. Never seen what?

NEUMANN. This has been smuggled into the country. Yes?

HANS. I /

FRED. / Christian?

NEUMANN. How else would it be here?

HANS. I've never seen it.

NEUMANN. So, it belongs to Anna?

HANS. I don't think it belongs to either of us. I've got no idea how it got in here. What was happening just now, when I came in? You were kissing her.

FRED. What?

DIETER *enters*.

What did you just say?

DIETER. Are we alright to come back down – we were worried we might wake Anna up?

HANS. She's awake.

DIETER. You feeling okay, love?

ANNA. I'm fine.

FRED. Christian? Answer me.

NEUMANN. Anna, will you come with me please – I'm going to need to have a conversation. Will you get your coat and shoes?

HANS. You can't walk my wife out of my flat because of a Western record.

DIETER. What's going on?

FRED. We listen to Western music all the time.

MARION *enters*.

MARION. Dieter?

NEUMANN. It wasn't just the record. She was packing a bag. When I came down here. she was in the bedroom packing a bag –

FRED *makes a break for the bedroom. NEUMANN stops her.*

FRED. If she was packing a bag, let's see it.

NEUMANN. The bag in which I found this record –

DIETER. It's only a record.

NEUMANN. And an American passport. In her name, with her photograph in it.

NEUMANN *shows the passports.*

ANNA *staggers slightly.*

HANS. Anna?

NEUMANN *blocks HANS from getting to her.*

MARION. This isn't right. Something isn't right, Herr Neumann.

NEUMANN. Frau Weber, please stop playing the victim. Will you go and get the bag please in which I found this record and the American passport? We need to leave.

ANNA *doesn't move.*

I'll go and get it for you.

ANNA *goes into the bedroom.*

77

MARION. I've known Anna a very long time. She's been a Party member for years.

DIETER. She's never flinched.

NEUMANN. Well maybe you don't know her as well as you thought.

The door bursts open. SOPHIE and KARL burst in, wrapped up from the cold and full of the joys.

KARL. She's right they're amazing.

SOPHIE. There were so many colours and these three guys down on the street were cheering up at us and we were cheering down at them – then we went down, and they gave us beer cans! (*Raises her beer can to the sky.*)

MARION. Yes, love.

KARL. She said she'd be my girlfriend!

SOPHIE *suddenly notices the atmosphere. Looks at ANNA.*

NEUMANN *checks the window – and the corridor.*

NEUMANN. Have you seen Schmidt? Was he on the roof?

FRED. What are you doing? She's my best friend. Were you kissing her?

ANNA *packs a bag.*

ANNA *reappears into the room.*

DIETER. Hans, you can't let this happen. You have to stop this. Do you know what they'll do to her. Hans?

HANS. I'm thinking. Stop talking. I'm trying to think.

SOPHIE. Frau Weber, you said you were going to sleep. Are you okay? Did you have a good sleep?

NEUMANN. Anna, will you come with me please?

ANNA. The fireworks are finished now.

ANNA *makes for the door with NEUMANN.*

HANS *steps in their way.*

HANS. Recently, Anna hasn't been feeling very well. She's not been sleeping. I get up in the night and she's padding about. She's not there. When I go and speak to her she's hiding things before I can see what they /

ANNA. / Hans. Remember.

HANS. She's just been a bit, unsure, nervous – she's always thinking someone is following us when they're not.

ANNA. Hans? Remember!

HANS. Our friends ring and she picks up the phone. She says no one is there, but I've heard them on the other end, I've been able to hear them /

ANNA. / Stop, stop.

NEUMANN. Move.

The sound of the elevator.

HANS. What I'm saying is, I don't think she's a traitor. She's not very well.

NEUMANN. She has an American passport.

HANS. Someone could have seen she was feeling a bit strange and taken advantage of that. Do you understand what I'm. Someone must have made her do it. Someone must have done it to her. She's not a threat to anyone – she's just unwell.

SCHMIDT enters.

NEUMANN. Schmidt, Hans has just made it clear that Frau Weber needs some help. We're going to get her that help as quickly as possible. Will you help us downstairs?

DIETER. Anna. Say something – Anna?

FRED. Anna?

HANS. You cannot walk my wife out of my flat!

NEUMANN. Karl? Keep everyone here.

79

KARL *nods, unsure.* HANS *goes for the door –* KARL *stops him.*

HANS. Get off me.

KARL. He said.

NEUMANN. Schmidt? Schmidt?

HANS. She didn't do this. I know my wife!

SCHMIDT. You're not going anywhere Max.

NEUMANN (*muttered*). Max? What? What are you talking about? We need to leave, now. Anna?

ELENA *in with the case.*

ELENA. Because you're in a terrible rush to meet your American friends at the border?

NEUMANN *looks about him.*

NEUMANN. Schmidt, I thought I asked you to take Elena home.

DIETER. What's going on?

ELENA. Folks, your new boss is – as Anna tried to explain – actually called Max Becker and he planned, this evening, to take Anna across the border into the American sector. The passports, the record – they're his. Anna's case – I imagine – has nothing in it.

ANNA *opens it.*

– has nothing in it.

NEUMANN. This woman has lost her mind. Hans – you need to – Schmidt? Schmidt!

NEUMANN *tries to run for the door – they slam him against the wall.* SCHMIDT *takes the passports out of* NEUMANN'S *pocket. He hands them to* ELENA.

ELENA. We have your confession on tape, Max. The planned escape, the American friends. We have all of it.

Beat.

NEUMANN. You betrayed me.

ANNA. Schmidt would you help Herr Neumann down to the car?

NEUMANN. You love me, and you betrayed me.

ANNA. I think he's feeling a little confused. Maybe you could give him something to help him sleep?

HANS. The pills –

SCHMIDT. Aspirin.

DIETER. Jesus, Anna.

SCHMIDT. Let's get you to the border and see if you can point out your liaison, shall we?

NEUMANN. Traitor.

ANNA. Did your Western friends buy you an expensive beer and watch the little socialist animal taste the wonders of their world?

ELENA. What the West doesn't realise, Max, is that capitalism is only a stepping stone en route to socialism. Their arrogance will see them falter. Soon they will need to believe in something bigger than themselves or they won't survive.

NEUMANN *laughs – disbelieving her idealism.*

ANNA. Did you slip and leak and spill yourself everywhere, Max?

NEUMANN. I did it to save you.

81

ANNA. Why would I want to go to a country where you're pushed to spend money you don't like earning on things you don't even want? Where you go from the dignified position of having your needs met to having things forced on you all the time, like a dog that can't say no. It's humiliating.

NEUMANN. You had a hard time saying no yourself, as far as I remember.

DIETER. Hans!

HANS *goes for MAX. People restrain him.*

SCHMIDT. Frau Hillenbrand, we need to get Neumann to the border to see if he can point out his liaison.

NEUMANN. The photo of Anna on your desk. Did she ask you to put it there?

HANS *doesn't respond.*

So you don't know her that well, then, do you?

HANS *looks at ANNA. Doesn't respond.*

MARION. Anna.

NEUMANN *is removed by* SCHMIDT.

ELENA *approaches* ANNA.

ELENA. Well done, darling.

ANNA. For Mama.

ELENA. For your country. Im Herzen Wahrheit, im Geiste Klarheit.

ANNA. The recording?

ELENA. Just here. It's ready. Can you bring back the equipment as soon as you're done? (*To the room.*) She's an example to us all.

MARION. What's happened to Robert? Will he be back?

ELENA. We had to make some space for Herr Neumann, so Robert took a little holiday. He's back on Monday. He's looking forward to seeing you all. He's been impressed by your loyalty. You all took to your new boss so quickly, especially you Hans.

ELENA exits.

Silence in the room.

KARL. You let that doctor in here knowing what he's /

MARION. / Keep your mouth shut. No one say anything.

SOPHIE grabs her coat, terrified by what she might have said – and runs out.

KARL *leaves, going after* SOPHIE.

Dieter? Come on.

ANNA. Marion? Listen to me.

MARION. Okay. That's fine. Thank you for the party.

DIETER (*looks at* ANNA). I've known you for years.

MARION. Dieter.

DIETER. You're like a daughter to me.

MARION. Stop.

84

MARION *pulls* DIETER *away.*

DIETER. No point being quiet now, we've spilled our guts all evening without having a fucking clue. Haven't we? Your fucking favourite?

ANNA. I had to, they asked and I couldn't say no.

DIETER. Yes, you could. I did.

ANNA. And look what they've done to you.

DIETER. Yeah, I've been stuck for years. I'm an embarrassment. The tragedy of Dieter. But who cares, because we are nothing if we're not good to each other.

ANNA (*weakly*). He was a traitor. Herr Neumann was a traitor.

MARION. Goodnight.

MARION *grabs* DIETER – *and marches him out of the room.*

DIETER *tries to return.*

Get out. We've got children.

MARION *returns, squeezes* HANS *on the shoulder.*

I'll see you on Monday. Let me know if you need anything.

MARION *and* DIETER *leave.*

ANNA *tries to stand strong – but it's killing her.*

ANNA. I was trying to keep us all safe.

ANNA *turns quickly – spots* FRED, *but she's already up – on her way out.*

I didn't know. I didn't know he'd gone after you, I swear. Not until this evening – we didn't know he'd been staying with you /

FRED. / He told me he loved me.

ANNA. Maybe he did?

Beat.

FRED. Don't lie any more than you've already had to.

FRED *leaves.*

HANS *sits, watches.*

ANNA *gets the suitcase and opens it – and puts it on the table.*

ANNA *stumbles, she's shaking.*

ANNA *makes sure HANS is listening.*

ANNA *presses play.*

The recording:

> ANNA. That's not love. Love makes me happy. That's – ego. It makes, it'll destroy you.
>
> MAX. Tell me you haven't spent years wondering where I am.
>
> ANNA. I love my husband. I love our life.

ANNA *rewinds.*

> ANNA. I love my husband. I love our life.

ANNA *rewinds.*

ANNA. I love my husband. I love our life.

Beat.

HANS. Made sure you said all the right things?

ANNA. I never lied. Not once.

HANS. You told me who he was, and I didn't believe you.

ANNA. I didn't think you would. He was your boss.

HANS *presses play on the machine.*

The recording:

MAX. But do you want your husband?

ANNA. You can't build a country on want.

Pause – HANS *looks at* ANNA.

Well you can't. Can you. I did it for us. I wanted us to be safe from…

HANS. From you wanting him?

Pause.

Can they still hear?

ANNA *reveals the wire that is on her person.*

It's on your body.

ANNA *nods, timidly – goes towards* HANS *in some way – touch/hug –* HANS *can't allow it.*

ANNA *takes the cable that links her pack to her headphones and she holds it in one hand, she pulls the cable out. She takes the bug off her person.*

HANS *watches the apparatus come apart.* ANNA *puts it on the table.*

Our ears go into white noise. We can't hear a thing. ANNA *shows* HANS *that she's disconnected it.*

Do you feel better? Do you?

ANNA *approaches* HANS – HANS *can hardly look at her.* HANS *walks away from her.*

In silence.

ANNA. Hans. Hans!

HANS *goes into the bedroom, closes the door.* ANNA *stares forward.*

The End.

87

www.nickhernbooks.co.uk

facebook.com/nickhernbooks

 twitter.com/nickhernbooks